# Real Talk

A Journey to Faith, Hope, and Love.

ISBN: 978-0-692-05530-4

For the hearts that run over with love.
Thank You.
To my loving and supportive mother, your drive will forever be
inspirational to me.
Love you! ♡

# CONTENTS

Meet the Author     i

About me                         1

Honestly                         7

Broken                           9

The Power of Affirmations        26

Goddesses Only                   35

Man, He's Fine                   47

I Can't Do This Alone            57

Love of My Life                  75

Heart to Heart Letter            92

# Meet the Author

**Shakira Rayann Pierre-Louis** is a sixteen-year-old author, motivational speaker, and mentor. She is also the founder of P.O.M.S. (the Power of Motivational Self Confidence), a program that incorporates cheer and dance to promote the idea of self-love and confidence to young girls. Holding the title of Miss Jr Teen DC United States 2016, Shakira continues to promote the power of self-love to young women across the United States.

# About me

"Once upon a time. . ." documents the beginning of every fairy tale ever told. You know, the fairy tale you heard of as little girl, ones like, the flawless tale Cinderella, the unconditional love of The Princess and the Frog, and the infamous Beauty and the Beast. A one-sided perception of beauty was instilled in me from a young age, forcing me to believe that beauty is rare, gifted only to royalty. We were trained to think that we were broken damsels in distress, waiting for a prince to save us. Young girls were deceived into viewing young men as their salvation, constantly searching for the validation of a man to determine their self-worth. When these same young girls were introduced to the reality of the world, their hearts were broken, and their self-esteem plummeted. As you read the content of this book, I want each and every one of you gems to create your own fairy tale. However, in this majestic tale, the princess will save herself; never again to be a damsel left in distress.

Before I assist you in creating your own fairy tale, I want to begin with my story. My story, like most fairy tales, is a love story. The same love that is raved about in fairytales, idolized in movies, published in books, and spread amongst your dearest friends and family; all begins with yourself. My fantasy of love was quickly tainted, when persecution from my peers lead to the plummet of my self-esteem. My story of being bullied began around the age of twelve. This would, in essence become a part of my life's story.

Entering middle school, I was extremely ecstatic, slightly nervous, and nevertheless, eager to take on the world. At this age, I was completely unaware that individuals could be disliked without reasonable explanations. My idea of kindness and generosity was quickly tainted when I began to experience persecution from my peers; ultimately leading to a decline in my self-esteem. Small remarks quickly escalated to vulgar insults about my character and appearance. Rumors were created, which prevented me from walking past groups of girls without someone pointing, laughing, shouting, or staring at me. Having no friends to confide in, I would often spend my lunches in solitude, in the media center or locker room. My school days were spent in silence. Desiring not to be seen, I believed that it was less painful to be ignored than humiliated. My joys were vigorously ripped away, as my easily influenced mind was flooded with the opinions of my surrounding classmates. The reflection of myself had been molded into someone that was too dark, too skinny, unintelligent, flawed, and insufficient.

After endless nights of tears streaming from my eyes, I was bestowed with the biggest blessing of mankind, I had developed a new mindset. Moving forward I decided to no longer let others determine my identity. Taking the steps toward self-love, I created an affirmation board declaring all the things I wanted to be. Over the course of time, my reflection, which was previously seen as ugly, became the most beautiful image to me. I had developed a deep passion for encouraging others to incorporate self-love into their lives. Given the opportunity to enter a beauty pageant, I was overjoyed. The pageant greatly motivated me to get involved in my community. I swiftly created a program, using cheerleading and dance to teach girls to uplift one another rather than allow their competitive nature to deteriorate their peers. The P.O.M.S. (Power Of Motivational Self Confidence) program won the hearts of the judges, crowning me Miss Jr Teen DC United States 2016.

Not only would I be given the chance to conduct my program as a titleholder, but pageantry gifted me with the opportunity to become a motivational speaker, mentor, and coach for the organization G.I.R.L.S. (**G**ifted, **I**ntelligent, **R**esilient, **L**oved, and **S**uccessful). I love to help, heal, and mend the hearts of others. I make it my daily goal to spread love, kindness, and compassion to as many individuals as possible. Four years ago, when I sat on the locker room floor all alone, I was completely unaware that every insult hurled at me would be the stepping stone that I took to accomplish my dreams. Every individual that attempted to belittle me, equated to every young girl that I encouraged to grow. If only I knew so long ago that I'd someday turn my pain into passion, what a wonder it would have been. I am thrilled to be able to share with you all of my tips, so that you may finally become the ruler of your own destiny. Feel free to sit down, grab a snack, and get comfortable; because this is real talk.

# Honestly

I am not a teacher, nor is this a lesson.
I am simply just sharing
The secrets and blessings of life.
That God has given me.

# Broken

Empty words.
Empty words flood through my head.
I have become too accustomed to pain.
I am too familiar with the rigorous rhythms of abuse.
It seems as though even compliments are only capable of
amounting to empty words.
This endless ocean of reassurance is given to you.
In this crystal clear ocean swims the gentle words, "I love
you."
Bountiful statements uttering, "I care,"
and the infamous song ringing in your ear.
"I will never leave you."
Yet somehow. . .
These potent promises topple over into a pile of dust.
Empty words have a habit of sticking around, desiring to
never leave your side.
And subsequently leading to a leech of despair that sucks all
of the joy from your life
Everywhere you go.

Over the years.
Over the years she cried,
"Love me" desperately wanting your attention.
Over years she begged
"Love me!" dying for your tender affection.
"Love me . . ." she whined tired of repeating herself.
"Love me," she scoffed, mocking the idea of love in itself.
Over the years she finally screamed.
With a smile radiant in her cheeks and tears flooding her
eyes.
"Love me!"
After all these years she discovered her self-worth,
Realizing exactly how to, "love herself."

Honestly, it's okay not to be okay. This is normal. You do not have to be perfect, joyful, and social every single day of your life. Some days you may just want to keep to yourself and that is okay. Your worth has not decreased. Your value as a person has not been diminished. You are still beyond amazing if you have an off day. Some days you will wake up and simply decide to take a break from the rush of things. Don't feel forced to put on a facade that you and I both know is not genuine. Take a break. Take a breather. And relax. Just remember this is only some days. After taking the day off, remind yourself that you deserve happiness. Remind yourself that you are in control of your life. Remind yourself that everything in this life is ranked in your favor. Even the aspects of life that you may not seem to quite understand. After hitting the pause button on your life, after the intermission from your daily, please don't forget to hit resume.

The storm. The storm that grazes my soul and caresses my heart. The storm that is deathly deafening, vibrantly fearless, and never spears mercy. THIS STORM. This storm has a way of demolishing my home, where all the comfort and safety of my mind lay their head at night. Screaming in rage, sick and tired of the rain; I pack my bags and race to the door and then....

BOOM!

Thunder.

Thunder came and erupted in my brain, shifting the principles that once kept me sane.

And through all the thunder I can somehow manage to hear a silence. A silence that is oddly familiar to my ears. It is the same silence I became acquainted with every time, every individual whom I thought I loved simply walked out of my life. Leaving me shattered with the same bruises gagging deeper into my skin, and scaring me. Then there was a murmur in the distance, but all I could hear was the storm! There was a murmur in the distance, it was a voice crying out to me. LISTEN! LISTEN! LISTEN TO ME! This voice was crying out to me trying to get a hold of me through this storm. FOLLOW ME, PLEASE uttered the voice.

But I refused. I was too scared to go out into the storm. So, I put on my headphones and blasted the radio trying to despairingly block out this storm. Because it is more comfortable to sulk in the pain than to deal with the storm. But my dear queen, just because you block out the storm doesn't mean that the rain will go away. And until you begin to look at the reality and see that there is a gloomy cloud living above your head, the thunder will only get louder. And unless you decide to choose bravery over fear and knowledge over ignorance; your storm may never fade. Dear beloved queen, storms are not meant to last forever. Storms are designed to fade away. You must choose to walk through the rain. Because somewhere between this rock and hard place where you reside; a rainbow remains. Waiting for your arrival. Just walk through this storm day by day, and eventually the undeniable beauty of life will unravel, and an everlasting rainbow will be portrayed.

Betrayal, deceit, and pain is common in this world. However, you must avoid these conditions like the plague. Be wary of people's actions, as these characteristics will reveal their true intentions. Ask to be graced with discernment. For with this spirit you are enabled to find even the dullest pin resting in what may seem to be a comfortable stack of hay.

Sometimes we'd rather be comfortable in the path of the world then to step out on faith and trust the path that God is creating for us. Stop trying to reopen doors that God has obviously closed. Aka sis MOVE ON. There will be better.

~Note to self

Jealousy and envy. Understand Dear Queen that you are not in competition with those surrounding you. THEIR victory does not mean YOUR defeat. You are uniquely made. Although one girl may be able to perform a certain craft effortlessly, no one can perform that task the way you do. Thus, giving a chance for everyone to gain the victory. For each person's purpose is unique. Be bold Dear Queen, and know that you are enough. Know your worth and do not fear those around you. This will keep your heart from turning bitter and spiteful towards others. We are all human. If success can be granted to her, you have the ability to obtain success.

Stay encouraged. It's true, sometimes you will break. Sometimes life leaves you hopeless, emotional, and on the breaking point of going crazy. These feelings are okay. It is okay to have these emotions, however do not let them consume you. The problem with a broken vase is not that there are cracks in the glass. The issue arises when you choose to become too comfortable in your broken ways that you remain sulking in pain. You choose to leave the broken pieces sprawled all over the place. It is perfectly normal to have bad days, this is fine. Just do not get stuck in that cycle of life. Stay encouraged Dear Queen, do not say, "I am sad," as there is too much power in that phrase. Instead state that, 'the situation that I am placed in makes me feel sad,' so that your words will not define you. You are going to be more than fine in the end, regardless of how broken things may seem. Speak it into existence.

For years I had believed that only certain people were deserving of love. I was not aware that affection and intimacy should be given to everyone. My naive mind had a preconceived notion that you must reach a particular standard of perfection for love to find you. I later realized that this is not true. Love is not built for the perfect ones. Love meets you right where you are. Love is ready to embrace everything that you are and everything that you aspire to be. You do not have to force love to find you, nor do you have to force love to stay. There is someone for everyone. And someday you'll meet the one for you.

I am not irreparable. I will not be labeled as broken or damaged, just to be thrown away.
My wounds can be repaired. This pain is not permanent.
Believe me.

Cry.
Reflect.
Live on.
You will conquer this.
Just go through the healing process.

The Past: a lesson to be learned, often left as a memory. Never defining your destiny.

The Present: Only lasting for a second. Do not get engulfed in the thrill of the moment, believing that these seconds will last for eternity.

And never forget.

The Future: Whatever you want it to be.

I never WANTED to be her.
You simply weren't acknowledging me.
And I adored the attention she received.
So I tried to mimic her characteristics, thinking maybe people will love me.
It destroyed me to think that they would never love me.
The real me.
And all my authenticity.
So I chose her.
Only because it was easier.

I know. You're not everything they wanted you to be. Cry about it and let the hurting out. And when you're done, wipe your tears. Now it is time to start following your dreams. After all, you have your own destiny. And they were simply blocking a vision that would someday reveal itself to be a reality.

I wanted you.
Each and every one of you.
I had love for you.
But you obviously didn't have love for me.
Because when I was begging for attention no one ever
seemed to notice me.
You didn't even see the tear than ran down my cheek.

I have been crying for a long time. My tears ran over creating oceans of salty bitterness. My pain stretches across the galaxies of time and space. Insecurity grasped my throat slowly strangling me. Until now. That girl you saw before is no longer me. You can take the pieces of her heart and crumble them as you choose to, because SHE is no longer attached to me. I am walking away from my past and beginning my journey to healing and victory.

Cheers to me. And the woman God created me to be.

# The Power Of Affirmations

Every morning and night, repeat these words to yourself.
I am loved beyond belief
I am loving and kind
I am enough
I am financially abundant
I am positive and happy
I am full of feminine energy
I am joyful and vibrant
I am strong and powerful
I am intelligent and wise
I am beautiful now and forever more
I am incredibly blessed
Everything on this Earth is ranked in my favor
I am everything I've ever wanted to be
And I am complete

Dear Queen, let these words manifest into your reality.

Imagine a pink hat. It's perfectly crafted nature has been alluring your eyes for years. This luxury cap is worth the world to you. The design of this cap is so expensive, you would currently have to sell all of your belongings just to make a down payment on this accessory. However, regardless of the circumstances, your heart is set like stone on this pink hat. You say to yourself, "That pink hat will be mine" and the Universe replies, "your wish is my command." Unconsciously you send messages to the Universe claiming ownership to the pink hat by affirming your desires. And as if the Universe is simultaneously intertwined with your thoughts, your fantasy becomes reality. You wake up one morning, and walk outside to check the mail. In your mailbox this magnificent pink hat is bestowed flawlessly. Almost as if it was waiting for you all along. This is the power of affirmation. Or a higher terminology for this ideology the law of attraction.

She was absolutely beautiful; incredibly stunning from head to toe. It wasn't her looks that mesmerized my eyes and melted my heart, but rather her virtuous soul that captured my attention forever. She's powerful, swaying her hips when she walked. She was Spiritual, attracting only the positive energy of this world. Her smile could warm even the coldest hearts. Her lively energy was uplifting. . . even on the darkest days. Conversationalist at the least, as her charming words are music to all ears who were listening. She was productive in her purpose in life, never taking a day for granted with the utmost gratefulness. She was a leader to all of those that followed. Her silly remarks and goofy character brought about laughter into a room. Wise as can be, she spoke with few words, however every word held great importance. Who is this girl? Sounding like every girl's life goals and every man's fantasy. The woman that I am speaking of is you. You are this woman, as you come in different sizes, shapes, shades, and even faces. These characteristics may vary from person to person, but the essence of the individual remains the same. Speak it, believe it, and receive it. You are a dream girl. YOU are the person you admire the most.

I can, and I will. Point. Blank. Period.

Every person on this Earth holds energy.

And there is always a response to the energy you output into the world.
Some of which is positive energy.
Some of which is negative energy.
Energy is generated from thoughts, feeling, and general emotions.
The vibes you carry transfer to each and every individual you meet.
Your energy draws in circumstances, in which you must endure.

Scenario: Imagine you woke up late one morning. Rushing to begin your day, your energy was thrown off due to annoyance of your tardiness. Because you have such negative energy, you set yourself up to encounter additional issues consisting of bad vibes. As you rush to exit the house, you spill coffee of your favorite work shirt. With bubbling anger, you hop in your car, slam the door, and begin to drive to work. After finally reaching your destination with five minutes to spare before you must clock in, you encounter a jerk who stole your signature parking spot. Infuriated and fed up you get into a full-blown argument with this individual lasting for what may seem like eternity, ultimately making you 20 minutes late to work.

Dear Queen, your negative energy simply attracted people and circumstances with energy similar to the one in which you were portraying. Rule of thumb, if you want to attract positivity produce good vibes only.

You have the power to create your own destiny.

Understanding the concept of attraction.
If you desire to attract greatness.
You must align your feelings, thought, and speech with that goal.
Understand that everything in life is ranked in your favor.
You have purpose, and you have been placed on this Earth to succeed.
See every scenario as a blessing regardless of the difficulties.
Although you may not see the benefit of your struggle currently;
Eventually your dry season will become a harvest.
And surely this will be a bountiful feast!

Sometimes you have to encourage yourself, even when it seems as though the simple task of breathing is too much of a difficulty. Sometimes you have to dust dirt from your temple of life and adjust your crown of faith. Sometimes you have to speak victory over your life. It is easy to stay positive and joyful when life is bliss. The difficulty is permitted when the hardship arrives, but dear queen, regardless of your current feelings; speak the word of God over your life and you will be healed. Speak nothing but positivity over your life. Dear queen, remember your place. You belong to the royal family. Your light is too bright to be dimmed by the circumstances of this world. Let your glory shine on all of those who surround you. Shine like the diamond you were created to be.

You have yet to see how great your life can be.

Dear Queen, you are beginning to create your own destiny.
Bestowed with encouragement, power, and self-affirmations;
you will begin your journey to living your best life.
Never settle for less.
Chase each goal like it's your last.
Love with your whole heart unconditionally.
Laugh so that your smile may never fade.
Do not live just to live my dear love.
You are much too significant for merely existence in itself.
Live so that you can look back on this world as see an
imprint
I
Was
Here
You have control
You are living your best life.
Starting now.

# *Goddesses Only*

Often recognized as a form of validation in today's society, the standards of beauty has been distorted in the media reaching unrealistic target levels. Contrary to what is often practiced amongst women, caring for your appearance is a mannerism that is meant to appeal to only YOUR needs. Caring for your appearance is merely a way to maximize your comfort, maintain high spirits, and ensure your comfort level is at its peak. Similar to the classic proverbs, beauty comes down to the basic notion of, "You look good you feel good." Although lazy days, messy buns, and oversized sweatpants are a must every once in a while; maintaining aesthetics encourages women to be productive, feel productive, and produce positive energy for the day. When you neglect your image, often times you train your brain to believe you are still in 'sleep mode' equating to sluggish behavior and melancholy spirits. Everyday does not have to be a runway, however you deserve to feel your absolute best every day both physically and emotionally.

Thankfully caring for your aesthetics differs from person to person.
The aspect of beauty can include, but is not limited: skin care, hair care, diet, fitness, makeup, style, the good old fashion, 'smell goods' and budgeting. As we go through various methods and tips to care for your appearance, feel free to take any tips that you believe can assist you in your day to day life.

SKINNNNNN CAREEEEEEEEEEEEEE!!!!!!!!!!
Skin care is the foundation to any good makeup routine or to all the flawless natural days.
Coming from someone who used to struggle with acne, I have been through endless products and skin care methods. From oil cleansing, sensitive skincare, all-natural mask, drugstore oldies, and even high-end products; you name it, I've done it all! Now that my skin has cleared up, I stick to a simple skin care routine that never fails. I use a combination of three products and an additional makeup remover for my glam days. Keeping a simple skin care routine can be a lifesaver, especially for us busy girls. To keep my skin healthy and clear I simple remove my makeup from the day using micellar water, cleanse my skin using my favorite face wash, and moisturize. In the morning times to refresh my skin I spritz rose water and go about my day. Simple, easy and efficient. Thankfully, this skin care routine can work for all skin types. However, the products you use will determine the efficiency of this routine.

Majority of the "best" drugstore acne products contain harming agents that cause irritation to the skin, intensifying the pre-existing acne. When using these so called 'acne prevention' products; you are merely furthering the irritation of your skin; therefore, creating a dependency for the products are supposedly meant to clear your skin, ultimately forcing the consumer to seek for products geared towards acne prone. And the cycle for acne companies gaining a financial profit begins. The products you use in your skin care routine can vary, choosing the best combination of skin care products that work for you. An amazing website known as cosdna.org, displays each ingredient in your favorite skin products and reveals the irritation level, as well as the acne causing agents in each product.

Princess Tips

1. Throw on a silk robe when you're in the house! It'll boost your spirits and confidence even on a lazy day.
2. Listen to uplifting music! Have a playlist of all the songs that make you feel amazing.
3. Find a workout routine that works for you. Yoga, kicking boxing, or simply going to the gym. This will not only make you look good, but you will begin to feel amazing over the course of time. Pick a routine that you know you will remain consistent with.
4. Drink lots of tea. Tea has various health benefits; from stimulating your brain to clearing your skin.
5. DRINK WATER! What you put in your body will be displayed in your physical appearance. Imagine! Drinking water brings hydration to your skin, nails, and hair.
6. Do your makeup, maintain your hair, and throw on a cute outfit. Catering to your physical appearance will allow you to feel energized, in addition to boosting your confidence.
7. Keep your room clean. Have everything organized and nicely decorated! Buy some plugins or candles to keep everything smelling good.

What's in my bag?

- Lip gloss is a must to keep your lips glowing to the forever!
  - Or if you are a matte girl carry around the lip product you are wearing that day, so you always stay fresh.
- Ladies! We cannot forget that mini deodorant
- Lotion and body spray just in case life decided to get a little crazy!
- And if you're an acrylic girl like me, carry around a nail file, nail glue, and some bandages in the instance that any accidents occur and one of your nails decides it wants to sit this party out.
- Keep a few snacks on hand if your days are long or busy.
  - Trust me you'll be grateful you did.
- Wipes and hand sanitizer is great if you and germs aren't really the best of friends
- And gum is essential for obvious reasons

## Stay low and Glow

- Stop caring about them! Notifications and likes on social media does not validate you! Compliments are meant to enhance your day not make your day. Do not put so much worth into the opinions of man, for their opinions sway with the rhythm of the wind.
- Read more self-help books. From poetry and self-love to making money; life secrets are hidden between the paperback covers left of book shelves.
- Update your music playlist!!! Music is powerful so find songs that make you feel good.
- Get your grades up! I know it's hard, but you will surely reap the benefits of all your hard work.
- Stay positive and energetic! You attract the same energy you put out. As Queens we can only afford to send blessings our way.
- Change up your daily routine! A new you requires a fresh start. Switch things up a bit. Get ready in a different order in the mornings or unwind from the day with added step.
- Keep your nails slayed as often as possible.
- Get a part-time job and start saving your coin.
- Get a journal! This is a great way to document your growth, write down your goals, and get to know a deeper sense of yourself.

Hair Care!
Healthy hair is quite simple to achieve but I believe simplicity is the most difficult part. For some reason we often think hair care is this gigantic project. General tips for every hair type is to invest in a good shampoo and conditioner as this is the foundation of your routine. Incorporate deep conditioning into your hair regimen weekly. If you need additional moisture try hot oil treatments as this is a great way to revitalize your hair. In regard to styling, KEEP IT SIMPLE! The less you tamper with your hair the more it will grow. Find about three stable hairstyles that you can always rely on and stick to it. If you can make sure that these hairstyles incorporate little to no heat. This can include but is not limited to roller sets, bantu knots, flexi rods, braid outs, wash n go's, and pillow soft curlers. If you prefer to wear your hair straight just ensure that you are wrapping your hair at night and sleeping on a satin pillowcase. Damaged hair requires a little more TLC, in which protective styles would be a better option, giving time for your hair to grow out and give you a chance for a fresh start. Protective styles are also great for my lazy girls, or simple ladies who wish to see consistent hair growth. Sew ins, buns, braids, faux locs, and wigs are very effective protective styles when cared for and maintained properly.

I adore makeup! I think it is great for enhancing your beauty and dressing up! Every glam girl should have their go to makeup routine. For those of you who are absolutely clueless when it comes to makeup, this is a great routine to begin.

Brows: Try to begin with a brow pencil or eyeshadow as they are easier to blend.
Foundation: Apply the product as dots on you face to ensure even distribution then blend.
Concealer: CLEAN UP YOUR BROWS!! This beautifies the whole look by tracing your brows with concealer.
Eyeshadow: Find three pigmented stable colors and blend till your hands hurt :)
Powders: Both press powders and loose powders are adequate enough to get the job done. Choose one color the shade of your foundation and the other color mimicking your concealer shade.
Highlight: Pigmentation can make or break this look.
Lips: There is a lot of flexibility in this range. The product varies from chap stick and Vaseline to lip stains and liquid lipsticks.
Lashes: On an everyday bases mascara is amazing, however for a little extra glam pop on some lashes.

For a more visual understanding, search up different concepts on YouTube. My favorite ladies to watch when I first began to get involved with makeup were BeatFaceHoney and GlamTwinz334. As these ladies have demonstrated in various videos, don't be scared to use drugstore products. The most important part of makeup is the technique, which you will master with consistency and practice, not the products you incorporate.

Of course, the list of beauty tips and tricks can continue on endlessly, however I simply wanted to list a portion on the key components I use on a daily basis. Physical appearance is only a small portion of what beauty means to me.

Mirror Mirror on the wall. . .

When I strip you of your makeup, luxurious hair, expensive clothing, and overpriced manicure Who's the fairest of them all?
Dear Queen
Charm and beauty are left in vain
But a heart of pure love and kindness
Will be praised amongst them all

# Man, He's Fine

Shattered.
As you walk away from the loving embrace of the man you foolishly believed would someday be your husband, you can't help but to feel. . . shattered.
Anger and frustration boils through your veins because, WOW!
You did it again.
Your ignorance to love equated to the infatuation of a man that could only picture his future between your legs.
But his alluring demeanor, charming voice, and captivating looks had you falling so deep in love, you are too blinded to realize the games he played.
He was toying with your heart like his favorite video game, because pride reassured his mind that your heart was the game that he'd always amount to winning.

Beautiful queen. . . when? When will you realize that you are royalty? When will you learn that not every man deserves your precious jewel? When will you see it is impossible to expect a joker to help you rule a dynasty? Beautiful queen, no longer will you allow fools to sit at your throne.  No longer will you wait on your king, but rather you will become busy with your kingdom until the royal man arrives. Trust and believe in the process of life. Understand that every event occurs in perfect timing. Stop blaming yourself for the absence of a partner. Sometimes you have everything you need for love to manifest, but your lover is still growing into that amazing man you hope to someday meet. Be patient queen. Allow yourself time to flourish in this season of singleness. Instead of focusing your mind on finding "the one," allow yourself to become the person in which you desire to find. Be the person who you admire.

Before you jump through hoops to grab that cute guy's attention, think to yourself why is he so desperately desirable? His inconsistency drives you crazy, as he fluctuates in and out of your life. You are never quite sure if he cares, due to the fact that he only calls your phone once every two months. I know you're playing mind games, singing to yourself, "He loves me, he loves me not." If I can drop an ancient gem between just me and you, that man will only treat you how you let him.

After the breakup, don't go back. You and I both know very well there is nothing waiting for you there. Nothing but those empty lies, salty tears, the sour scent of betrayal, and the swindling idea of hope for a broken romance. After shattering a glass, you drop down to the floor crying. Trying to rekindle the pieces together, you only amount to cutting your hand on the sharp edges on the glass. Yet, your mind dismisses the pain because your heart desperately desires to hold that precious glass once again. However, this is not possible. Ladies, the only way to get over that man is to delete him from your life. Delete the bitter ties of his phone number, social media, and the various pictures left on your camera roll. Believe me, it's hard to move on when you're still holding on.

How to spot a player.

In truth, you can see them from a mile away.
They come packaged with confusions, the art of illusion, and a permanent smirk on their face.
He will never give you 100 % effort, time, or love.
He will cover you in insecurity, self-hatred, or jealousy.
A player will always be alluring, because he has been crowned a mystery.
Always keeping secrets, withholding information, and flowing of lies.
The best way to spot a player is easier than you may perceive.
When this man shows you the true colors of his character the first time,
You must believe everything you see.

So now you may be wondering, exactly how do you attract
Mr. Right?

Well, after coming to a realization that love only occurs in
perfect timing,
Then you can begin to manifest the love of your life.
The secret to finding love is to stop searching for it.
You search as if this love is hidden amongst the stars.
Rather than expecting relationships to complete your
imperfect nature
Understand that relationships are meant to compliment your
magnificence
Love and care for yourself.
Love yourself mentally, physically, spiritually, and
emotionally.
The love that is bursting throughout your heart, in which you
are so eager to share
Release.
Allow this love to overflow upon your life
When the self-love you have begins to radiate
You will begin to attract the love in which you desire.
When people see you positive and happy they can't resist
but to join in on the fun.
Your irresistible nature will become intriguing to all the
GOOD men surrounding you.
Dear Queen, you're glowing.

You find yourself constantly questioning yourself wondering, "Does he love me?" To answer such a complex question, it would be necessary for one to understand the definition of love. Love does not bring about confusion, envy, or destruction. Love will not FORCE about feelings of change, but rather encourage a desire to grow. LOVE. True love is both given and received, never to be found in one-sided relationships. It was love's gentle nature that held no judgment against your crooked smile and frizzy hair. It was love's unconditional kindness that had the power to heal the deepest wounds and gashes of your heart. This love we speak of is always forgiving, holding no record of wrong doings. Love will adore each and every flaw that you possess; finding the beauty in the least of you, and praising the best part of your character. It does not take a genius or an expert to understand the meaning of love. In order to comprehend the dynamics to love, all you must do is look to the one who created love. He is the highest king living up above all.

I am amazing not because they recognized me.
But because God created me.
Perfectly.
For such a time as this.
I am amazing because I can do all things in Christ who
strengthens me.
I am amazing because He lives in me.
Jesus Christ. The highest King, God almighty.
The ultimate miracle baby.
The definition of love.
You remind me of who I am, and what it means to belong to
someone as great as you.

Take your time with life. Do not rush into love. Especially, when you know your heart is not capable of producing intimacy. When they ask you, "Why don't you follow us? Why won't you let your heartbreak with us? Why won't you be like society and rush into the facade of a perfect relationship?" Reply and say, "Everyone is the same; and I am trying to do something different." When they question and inquire, "What exactly is it that you are waiting for?" Ease their mind, and respond by vocalizing, "This is not a race to the finish line. It is all...a...matter... of... timing..."

# I Can't Do This Alone

God did not come for the ideal man and the faultless being. Perfection is not His request. Christ died to be with the broken, wretched, and those whose lives have been construed into a mess. So please, Dear Queen, never see yourself unqualified for this dynasty. YOU are the daughter of the highest King. You have already been accepted into the royal family.

He cannot love you like God has.
Do not make man your God, or surely you will be
disappointed.
For even the best of man is as frail as breath.

Do not let your past determine your future. For God does not care about who you were. The Lord is busy focusing on who He will transform you to be.

Your job as a Christian is NOT to live a perfect life.
Your job as a Christian is to open up your heart to Christ and
let Him convert your
Deepest scars
Blatant flaws
And catalog of imperfections
Into a testimony that will move mountains.

Oh, how He loves us.

There is nothing that He placed His hand on, that I can't achieve.

No longer will I scream. No longer will I shout from the top of my lungs, "OOOOOO OOOOOUUUU!!! Choose me! Please pick me!" For I have finally realized, God has already chosen me. And that is all that matters.

The Creator of love. The Artist of victory. The Mastermind of money. The definition of happiness. Dear God, almighty. Trust Him. He holds all that you desire.

I laughed with no fear of tomorrow. My path is different. I do not follow the normal curve. Please do not bother to figure me out or understand me. I am not on the world's timeline. There is a miracle tattooed between the letters of my name. God is doing something in my life.

If you often find yourself in the same circumstance over and over again. God is speaking to you. There is a lesson He is trying to get you to understand, however you seem to continuously lose your grip of the concept. Life tends to follow a continuous cycle until we declare change to be a part of our destiny. Be attentive and reflect so that you may rise above your circumstance.

Be steady in the season that God has placed you in. There is a reason the Lord has placed you there. Although your season may be flooding with tests and trials, and it may seem as though this season is too painful to live through; you must understand your muscles must tear before they grow. That is how you gain strength. Stop running when things don't go your way every time. Be still He said. Be still.

Every time you run away from God, you are running into the devil's territory. Have your armor ready because only war occurs there.

He is not always meant to be understood.
We are His children and He is our Father.
We need not engage in, "Grown folks' business."

The most intelligent man to walk the earth cannot even
understand the foolishness of God.
The strongest man to ever live cannot defeat God as his
weakest.
He is omnipotent.
With HIM on your side, the world is your playground.
Feel free to dance in your victory.

Love conquers hate. Every. Single. Time.

Let's be honest
I belong to only one.
I may not be a straight A student or have Barbie doll features
I may not be good at everything
But I am definitely great at some.
Regardless of such, I belong to One
So, no matter how this world chooses to depict me
Or makes fun of which category of life seems to fit me
I will always serve only one
And he will love me no matter what
Despite how tall, short, skinny, or fat I may be
He loves me
Despite the endless bruises that are left on my heart
That scream in anger and pain
At every individual who attempts to touch my heart
He loves me
My God will always be there for me
He kisses my head at night and tells me how much he
misses me when I am away
Entertaining the fantasies of all those worshipping the sun
He STILL loves me
So, every time you tell me time is ticking
Or I am behind in life
Stating that, "I cannot seem to amount to anything"
I laugh!
Those standards do not define me, you must not understand
In HIS eyes I am a miracle baby
Now and Forever
I belong to only one

Do not be overwhelmed with all that I have told you.
If you do not know God,
and desire to know Him like He knows you.
Breathe.
Simply say.
Dear God,
I need you desperately.
My heart is broken, and I heard you were a savior.
Please enter my life and save me.
Lord I accept you as Savior over my life.
As God Almighty.
Amen.


From here on out, there are only two things you must do.
Love God with your whole heart and love your neighbor as
God has loved you. Congratulations! You are now a part of
the Lord's family.

# The Love of My Life

The love of my life,

Is me.

Be kind to yourself
And kindness is what you'll receive.
But dear queen master the aspect of self-love
And your life will become a fantasy.

Shakira Rayann

I am in love with me.
And everything I have the potential to be.

Honestly, I'd be lying to you if I told you that life is going to be perfect.
Because this simply, is not true.
Sometimes you will struggle.
Sometimes you will find yourself facing extenuating circumstances
with an outcome in which you had not anticipated.
Life may not be perfect, but it is amazingly beautiful!
Do not let life run you around.
Do not allow life to tell you what your reality may be.
YOU take control.
You get to choose exactly what your reality will be.
Every single time.
Choose change over comfort.
Choose faith over fear.
Choose peace over destruction.
Choose happiness.
Every single time.

Happiness is a choice. A choice that may not always be easy. But this choice is SO worth it.

Happiness is a choice that requires effort constantly. You must put intentional time into ensuring that your happy meter is fulfilled. You must put your happiness first. You cannot cater to anyone else with your full capability if you are neglecting yourself. Dear Queen, always choose happiness and authentic joy. For every outburst of laughter you release, will surpass twice the amount of pain you felt with every tear. True happiness is so worth it!

My Radiant Morning Routine.
Every morning when you open your eyes, and God has graced you to see another day, be thankful. Gratitude is the first step to receiving abundance. You will never be given more if you do not value what you currently have. After emitted thankfulness into the world, you can now begin your day. It is essential that you reach an ultimate level of happiness before you even begin speaking to anyone. The goal is to allow your happy juice to reach its limit, so that if a circumstance or individual is able to disrupt your day; your juice is only partly strained. Problems emerge rather quickly, when your happy juice is left empty and the world decides to take a sip. Starting off your morning in a mediocre mood, gives ample room for outside factors to come in and snatch away the little happiness you had developed that morning. Ultimately, taking you from a glass half full, to a glass that is now empty. To avoid this complication, begin your day with a set of minor tasks that make you happy. Come up with a happy playlist of your favorite songs to listen to as you prepare for the day. Recite your list of affirmations. Make sure you have your favorite morning time drink that you know makes you do a little dance every time you take a sip. Fill your morning times up with simple events that will have you feeling fabulous as you walk out the door. Take time to do your hair, pick out a cute outfit that makes you feel comfortable and confident, and put on a little makeup if you are feeling fancy. This way you are ready to conquer the day and all that it has to offer.

Life works in season. There is a season of joy, pain, progress, and regression. Regardless of which, be grateful for the season you are placed in. Each season comes with a lesson and a hidden blessing. You cannot expect to amount to a "greater" season of life with more blessing; if you cannot be grateful for the life that lies in front of you. Why would you be granted a life of prosperity, if you simply choose to disregard the blessings that lie in front of you. Your grace will remain hidden in the fear that you will neglect its significance; similar to the blessing in which you currently choose to ignore. You beg for a new season of life forgetting that each season of life has a new set of struggles and issues to overcome. When will you be satisfied? Do not be too steadfast to win the race that trip over the finish line, as you were too fixated on what lies ahead. No matter how small or large the blessing may be, everyone has something to be grateful for. For every dry season you endure will be fulfilled with a season of harvest. So be patient with the season you are in. Learn to grow in this season, love deeper, forgive faster, and become stronger.

Let them sleep on you. Don't bother setting an alarm clock or knocking on the door to give a gentle reminder either. During their hibernation, grow. Grow into a woman that is not beautiful for merely her looks, but a woman that is beautiful for that soul that lays underneath. Become a woman of kindness, virtue, and intelligence. Develop a tender love that will soften even the hardest hearts. Laugh with a smile that spreads joy and positivity throughout an entire room. Be charming and eloquent in your speech, enticing all ears who chose to listen. Then my dear queen, only then will they wake up.

Every day that you awake you have the opportunity to choose who you desire to be. Each day you're granted the ability to be a better individual than you were yesterday. Today can be a complete 180 from yesterday. The power all lies within your hands. It's all up to you. Choose wisely.

It is not my job to get you to like me. It is not my job to impress you. And it will never be my job to change myself to appeal to your needs. I present the version of me, to which of whom, I love! Whether you choose to accept or deny this reality is none of my concern.

Speak it into existence. Finally, I am becoming the change I want to see in this world. I am falling head over heels in love with the incredibly stunning person I have become. I love myself for everything that I am AND everything that I'm not. I'm infatuated with the beauty that God has created. I deserve the world. Truly. From this point on, I will not settle for anything less than I deserve. I may have been one to reason with in the past, but this is a nonnegotiable decision. Because as I had decided to believe all that you could potentially be and doubt every ounce of potential that was left with in me; I ultimately resulted in losing myself completely. A risk that I will no longer be threatened with. I choose me and my worth over all things. Every single time.

There is beauty in wasted time. Not the time lost itself, but the lesson that arose from the hours spent in vain. To discover that you are a queen, that must only be surrounded by royalty. Realize that it will take a king to rule your dynasty. To familiarize yourself with this new ideology, being wise with who you allow to sit on your throne. You don't need the attention of all the princes' in the nation. You only need the love of the prince that will be crowned as your king. For him you should wait, in which I'm sure he'll appreciate. So that his dreams and your fantasy can mesh together to create "our" reality. You deserve a real king, someone just as amazing as you! Learn from time wasted and re-elevate yourself.

Just because they do not acknowledge your beauty, does not mean that such beauty does not exist. Dear Queen, man forgets to acknowledge the sun that shines every day, however this does not take away from the significance that the sun has in its place. You are gorgeous, regardless of the attention or lack thereof you receive. Your true beauty lies underneath.

What is beauty? Well. . . it simply depends on who you ask.
Although the answer may vary from person to person, there
is one thing that should always remain true

You are as beautiful as your heart is.

So, make it as glamorous as diamond, rubies, and gold.

The most beautiful sight to withhold is a passionate woman. The glow in her eye and the excitement in her voice when she raves about a topic that she loves. The childlike smile that excites glee all over her face is irresistible. She is a beautiful creation.

The best way to get in tune with yourself is to find a passion that you adore. Get involved in a way where you can leave a mark on the world. Even if it is just a small one. Spend your days in utter happiness doing what you love.

Often times as young ladies we have an idea of what we want "the one" to look, talk, or even act like. We spend all our time waiting for that perfect person to arrive. I want to shift your focus for an instant. If you choose to wait, why not wait intentionally. Instead of traditionally searching for "the one" take charge and become the person who you deeply desire to fall in love with. If you desire to be with a certain type of individual, you must put out a certain type of energy to attract them. People are naturally attracted to individuals who are likewise similar to themselves. Closing off our girl talk I want to give you all a task. Feel free to take as long as you need to accomplish this goal. Without thinking of any specific person in mind, create a mental or physical list of all the attributes you desire out of a partner. When you have finished the list go over and check off or highlight all the characteristics you currently possess. For the remaining characteristics think about how you can incorporate these personality traits into your daily life. Begin to slowly incorporate the various characteristics that you desire in a partner, which you are currently lacking. Allow yourself time to grow into the person in which you deeply desire to fall in love with. This will be a major asset in establishing a foundation of self-love. And ultimately taking a step closer to becoming that person in which you admire.

# Heart To Heart

Dear Queen,

I hope you were able to connect, relate, break, love, and heal throughout this book. As you begin this journey to self-love and happiness, please remember the gems that have been dropped amongst you. Understand that life may not be perfect. But the reality of perfection is a dull lifestyle in which you should desire to take no part of. Understand that life is nothing short of amazing. Everything in this life is ranked in your favor. "You have the key to your own destiny." As we say our last goodbyes until next time, remember you are beautiful beyond belief. Know that you deserve to be treated as royalty. Remember your place, as you belong to a royal family. Know your worth, desiring to never settle for less. Remain strong enough to be vulnerable. Spread your positive energy to the world! Be bold, as your voice deserves to be heard. My dear queen you are loved. You are successful. You are the best. May God grant you blessing all the days of your life.

Faith. Hope. and Love. Always and Forever,
Shakira

www.ingramcontent.com/pod-product-compliance
Lightning Source LLC
Chambersburg PA
CBHW051735040426
42447CB00008B/1141